FRONT ROW CENTER 4

ERIK HILDEBRANDT

My old friend from the Red Baron Squadron Randy Brooks wringing out the Eclipse 400 in a fully aerobatic demonstration at Oshkosh.

DEDICATION

Dedicating a book for me has always been an odd privilege as a self-published author. This time each year (usually right around the holidays), I have to look back at the year spent producing these works and decide how to recognize someone specific or maybe a group of people. This year, I decided soon after I heard the news in July, that I would try to celebrate Alan and Jennifer Henley. By now, the most of our airshow family is aware of Alan's freak accident playing with Skylar and Brandon after supper one night, but for those who are not, Alan Henley sustained a life changing injury to his spinal cord that for now has robbed them all of his mobility and traditional freedoms.

For their long time friendship and contributions as a favorite airshow brother and sister to us all, I humbly dedicate FRONT ROW CENTER 4 to Alan and Jennifer, and Skylar and Brandon. On those days when you guys feel tired, may these pages remind you that you are all very much loved.

-Erik Hildebrandt

FRONT ROW CENTER 4

Published in the United States of America by:
Cleared Hot Media, Inc.
Stillwater, Minnesota
erik@vulturesrow.com
http://www.vulturesrow.com
651-336-7150
First Imprint
ISBN 978-0-9674040-7-3
Printed in CHINA

Two of my favorite images of the Aeroshell Team shot at Oshkosh. On the left is the 4-ship formation on one of their famous late day sponsor hops. On the right is Alan and Jennifer together forever over Lake Winnebago.

ACKNOWLEDGEMENTS

Besides all the usual suspects that make FRONT ROW CENTER possible, a few folks stepped forward and helped in ways that made my life not only easier, but safer too. Col. Mark Sheehan and Doug Rozendaal manned the controls of the newly renovated gray on gray camo O-2A used as an aerial station wagon, getting my gear and me to and from shows. It also pulls duty as an outstanding and super smooth platform to shoot from and has been the test bed for my latest aerial photography innovation, the MachPOD. To learn more about this amazing piece of gear Go to: www.machpod.com

This year, flying with the Blues was primarily orchestrated by Craig "Merlin" Olson, perhaps the longest serving Blue Angel pilot EVER... maybe not by consecutive years served, but in total time in type, I doubt anyone trumps Merlin. Thanks too of course to to Boss Mannix, a fellow Eastern Long Islander who fondly cherishes the subtle charms of the Boardy Barn. For the third time, I got to chase the Delta around a homefield practice in Pensacola with Len "Loni" Anderson, the former Blue Angel solo who still bags Blue jet hops living nearby in Navy reserve status. Thanks Loni, I promise to double bag my breakfast next time to avoid unplanned leakage.

On the West Coast, many thanks must be offered to CDR Greg "HyFi" Harrison, the Skipper of VFA-122 at Lemoore, for mustering a division of his finest Rhinos for our epic photo tour of the San Francisco Bay Area.   On that mission, a RIANG C-130J crew consisted of Aircraft Commander- Capt James Couture, Co-Pilot- Capt Brendan Duffy, Uber-Loadmaster- TSgt Kyle Gurnon and Crew Chief- MSgt Steven Kreshak with 143 AW Media Support- MSgt Janeen Miller. They made a cross country flight from their base in Quonset Point, RI to the Salinas air show in northern California and had enough time left over to refuel and lead the four-ship of Super Hornets on our photo mission of a lifetime.

Estelle Brown's journalism background allowed her to contribute not just by writing but with some photographs as well. She is quickly making a name for herself among performers seeking to maximize their public relations potential and sponsorship development.

Dave Nilsen is a lifelong naval and military historian, a gift that he credits to his late grandfather, Edwin D. "Easy Dog" Robinson, who was a Machinists Mate aboard Pacific Fleet S-Boats in the 1920s. He wrote several of the key chapters in this book with the kind of style that keeps history alive and makes learning interesting facts fun.

-Erik Hildebrandt

Jeff "Buster" Clyman flies right seat with longtime warbird pilot Jim Vocell in the World Airpower Museum C-47 Dakota over the beaches near where I grew up in Hampton Bays, Long Island. Without too much trouble, you can imagine those are the white sands of Normandy below as the Invasion Striped transport presses inland on D-Day.

Front Row Center - by any definition that's the best seat in the house. That's MY seat at every airshow I announce.

I've been enamored with airshows since my dad took me to see the Thunderbirds when I was 12. I got to peek inside a Thunderbird F-100 Super Saber, touched the pilot's flight helmet and wondered what it would be like to be flying one of those jets.

That's not unusual for a kid. And it's not unusual for an adult who walks around the static display area of an airshow, gawking at the hardware that a precious few get to fly. Flight is a phenomenon that captures our dreams. We look up at airplanes that fly over our homes. We go to airshows, often not fully understanding just how amazing the pilots and machines and aerobatic performances are. What we do understand is the passion that gets into our guts as we see the skydance, the grace, the power, even the violence of high-energy tumbling. Those of us who haven't been in combat begin to understand the majesty of the warbirds and the price that was paid so that we could be free to attend such a spectacular event.

We long to be in the cockpit - it's the Walter Mitty in all of us - wanting to throw the airplane through the sky and have people on the ground stand in awe, applaud, and whistle. We want to feel the G's pressing us into the seat, contorting our face, experiencing the freedom of leaving the ground. Until we have the airplane, the license, and the experience necessary, the thrill is vicarious - but no less real.

Those of us who are "on the circuit" experience that thrill almost every week. It doesn't go away after a long season - most of us go through "airshow withdrawal" until the shows start again in the spring.

Front Row Center is my antidote for airshow withdrawal. But whether you're an airshow fan or not, the images you're about to see will put you as close as you'll get to actually flying one of these magnificent machines. It doesn't matter what your age is. The thrill knows no age limits. It's up close and personal to the aircraft and people who fuel our dreams.

Front Row Center - now it's YOUR seat. Hang on.

-Rob Reider

Doug Rozendaal and Casey Odegaard taxi back to show center at Oshkosh in DUGGY, the familiar and unmistakable DC-3/C-47 owned by Casey's dad Robert Odegaard. Same plane as the previous page, different missions.

JULIE CLARK
Chevron MENTOR T-34

She is considered by many to be the "First Lady" of the airshow family, so it stands to reason that her T-34 Mentor mirror all the trappings of Air Force One.

Chevron

Standing at show center as Julie flies her routine provides for some up-close personal time with the underside of the CHEVRON Mentor T-34. Bottom left shows Julie as she counts blades during the cranking sequence of the T-28 TOP BANANA. Bottom right shows Julie saluting the "troops" along the show line at Oshkosh.

Pilots are by nature, high-achievers. From the first time you are trusted with the controls of an airplane, there is a dialog that begins inside your own head. It is a conversation between the part of you that wants to live through this challenging new test of skills and the part of you that is always urging you to reach a little beyond your grasp. It is a private little discourse that never really goes away. Even years after you have earned your wings, you are always checking in with yourself in the air to make sure that the survivor in you is on the same page as the thrill seeker. For Julie Clark, you can almost see that internal conversation going on as she rages around the aerobatic box during her deceptively named "Serenade in Red, White and Blue."

The truth is, Julie Clark has a very healthy and outspoken little voice in her head that is continuously trying to push the envelope of excitement when she is flying. While it seems to the uninitiated that her airshow routine is graceful, smooth and rigidly choreographed, those of us who have been around Julie for a bunch of years know first hand that her show is one of the more high-energy acts on the circuit.

First of all, what few people realize is that while the T-34 Mentor was conceived of and built as a primary trainer for the military, the designers intentionally made it a heavy aircraft on the controls. In order to prepare young new military pilots for the heavy fighters they eventually would be expected to master, the T-34 flight characteristics, while honest and favorable, were left somewhat unrefined and raw so as to require better piloting skills to develop early on in the flight training process. Coupled with a modest piston power-plant that

requires the pilot to stay focused on their location on the power curve, Julie Clark manages to leave spectators with the impression that her mighty Mentor is rocket powered and hydraulically boosted.

From the distance of the crowd line, what folks cannot really see is how hard Julie is actually working at manipulating the controls. The heavy G-loads exerted during her extremely tight maneuvers are difficult to envision because Julie executes the turns with such smooth precision that it almost seems natural for her plane to follow the lines that it does. In reality, longer sustained medium G-loads are actually far more difficult to withstand than momentary high G-loads typical of purpose-built aerobatic competition aircraft.

Ironically, it is the heavier gross weight of the Mentor that Julie uses to her advantage in the energy management regime of her routine. Because a body in motion wants to stay in motion, Julie converts high altitude at the beginning of her routine into high speed as she dives into the box with an air start. It is this down-hill jump start that gives the Mentor its boost of kinetic energy that Julie long ago mastered how to extend through her entire routine. By keeping her turns silky smooth and always trimming out the drag, Julie maintains a level of optimum performance from one corner of the aerobatic box to the other.

It was while shooting of the images of Julie that appear in this chapter that I began to fully grasp the level of exertion she goes through during the routine. At the Salinas International airshow in California, I was out at the show-center line with Julie's crew chief, Tony Filippi,

Opposite page shows Julie formed up tight on the Baron being flown by Doug Rozendaal near Julies Minnesota home base at Webster. This page top is looking up through the pyro as Julie circles to land at Salinas. Bottom right catches a moment of connection between Julie and her fans with whom she shares her inspiration.

HIT THE DECK! Tony Filippi and I dive for the dirt as Julie sets herself up for the star-burst pyro pass at the Salinas airshow. Opposite catches Julie as she climbs out of the T-34 at Oshkosh and then a break-to land in the T-28 over Minnesota.

who sets off the pyrotechnic charges (fireworks) at the end of her act. During the course of her maneuvers prior to the fireworks however, Julie was making low, overhead passes while coming out of vertical rolls and loops. It was during these passes that I finally got a sense of just how fast and how many Gs Julie was enduring for the 12-minute show.

As if that were not enough to prove her airmanship, Tony began firing fireworks right into the center of the airspace Julie uses to wrap up her turns and finally set up to land. Again, from the crowd line, the distance belies

the significance of the size of these mortar charges. The distance, combined with this all happening in broad daylight leaves spectators with the impression that these are practically theatrical "sparklers." Take it from me, they are not. As far as I could tell, these are the real deal like you see every 4th of July, and Julie flies just out of their reach. What does still reach her, is the blast as these four inch shells explode as she drops the gear and comes in to land.

Of the glimpses I caught of Julie from the ground as she flew by just a few feet away, I could see that the thrill

seeker voice in her head was driving the bus. If you ever have any doubt that this pistol-packing pilot is capable of handling the heavy iron, remember that Julie Clark only recently retired from her Captain's job in the left seat of the AIRBUS A320. And if you still need proof she is the real deal, take a look at these shots of Julie at the controls of her pristine T-28 Trojan. Now that is a military trainer purposely built to weed out the chaff and separate cargo pilots from the fighter jocks. Julie Clark is certainly no cargo pilot and when you get the chance to watch her next time, you will better understand why she is wearing a batter's glove in the cockpit: because when she swings that stick, you are going to see a home run!

The California girl banks over the Marin headlands north of the Golden Gate bridge on the opposite page. Julie addresses the crew as Tony and Shannon rig the T-34 with smoke at Salinas. This page shows Julie in her trade-mark salute with the flag as she gets towed back to the hot pits.

Julie rolls over the top as the pyro star-bursts mark the end of her dynamic and patriotic aerial tribute to America. Opposite page shows one last pass for the evening commuters heading home from San Francisco.

The Fighter Group of Warbirds Over Long Island

Bringing history to life and presenting it to people all around the country is the mission, it just so happens that this father and son formation are living their dreams in the process.

Essay By Doug Rozendaal

Chris Baranaskas leads his dad Bob on a early morning photo mission along the south shore of Long Island.

Chris saddles-up to go make a low-level run of the beach all the way out to the Montauk Lighthouse and back. On the opposite page, Chris formed up on the left side of the Skymaster to capture these pure-aft perspective shots from my remote aerial imaging system, MachPOD was mounted out under the left hand wing. This device gives me a B-25 tail gunner perspective for photography on an economical and hugely versatile platform in the Cessna 337.

During World War II, the skies over New York's Long Island were full of fighters. The majority of them built at the Grumman and Republic Aviation plants. While the WWII Warbird assembly lines are now quiet, the skies are still home to prowling Warbirds: those of "The Fighter Group" from Warbirds Over Long Island.

The Fighter Group was formed by the father-son team of Robert and Christopher Baranaskas and the classic fighters they pilot: the North American P-51D Mustang "Glamorous Gal" and Curtis P-40E Warhawk "Old Exterminator".

The senior Baranaskas learned to fly in 1969 in a Cessna 150, but building his career and raising four children with his wife Cynthia pulled him away from flying for nearly 20 years. During this time, Bob left his position as President of a national wine and spirit company to purchase a leading Kentucky Bourbon distillery with a partner. Bob and his partner were the creators of the original Single Barrel Bourbon Whiskey. The concept was a huge success and they eventually sold the distillery to an international beverage company. Today, Baranaskas and his son Chris own and operate The Fairoaks Group, a real estate development, building and management company on Long Island.

No longer commuting between New York and Kentucky, Bob's mind began to wander back towards aviation and especially the memory of his father, a former WWII fighter pilot and instructor. Bob looked for a connection with his father's past and found it in WWII aircraft. In 2000, Bob purchased a North American SNJ-5 Texan; the undisputed stepping stone for anyone looking to fly WWII fighters and the advanced trainer flown by nearly every US fighter pilot during the war to earn his wings. As Bob was returning to aviation, his son Chris was

Later the same day we all went back out with Jim Vocell and Scott "Buster" Clyman in the C-47 seen in the first pages of the book. This shot is a great study of liquid sheet metal and late afternoon light. The shot was taken just offshore of the Shinnecock Inset where I grew up surfing.

starting his trip towards flying Warbirds; becoming the third generation of Baranaskas men to fly WWII fighters.

In 2001, when he was 21-years old, Chris began flying the SNJ-5 to airshows all over the Eastern US. Today most pilots checking out in the T-6 are older, with hundreds, if not thousands, of hours in their logbooks. Chris' experience was more typical of a WWII pilot, the Stearman, Texan, Mustang path. "It is hard to believe the veterans did it (flew the SNJ) with less experience than I had, and then they went off to combat, a truly remarkable feat", says Chris.

After completing the time requirements in the SNJ-5, Chris transitioned to the P-51 in 2005 by completing a check out and training program with Lee Lauderback at Stallion 51. Lee runs the most rigorous training facility in the world and it is the only place to go for training in the P-51.

With Chris moving up to the P-51 Mustang, Bob took the opportunity to move into the P-40 Warhawk. Now with two high performance fighters, the father and son team began putting together a two-ship demo for airshows around the mid and Eastern U.S. Both aircraft are crowd favorites and during the 2008 season each were flown in the prestigious USAF Heritage Flight Program with Dale "Snort" Snodgrass and Ed Shipley acting as pilots.

Bob says, "The role Warbirds play is displaying our heritage from a wonderful time when our country was united for a single cause."

"At the airshows, we meet pilots with tears in their eyes who flew these airplanes during the war. For many of the veterans it is the first time in over sixty years since they have

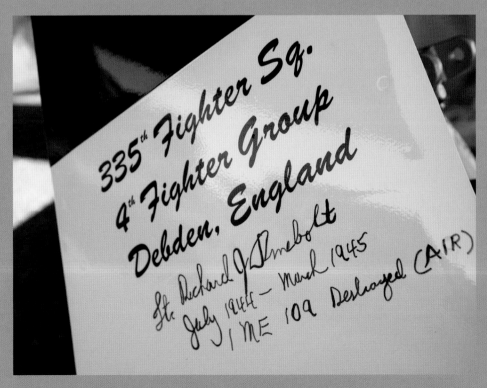

Bob Baranaskas catches the beautiful last light of fall over the Atlantic ocean as the moon rises in the east. Opposite page shows Bob ready to crank and the Warhawk leading the Mustang in a backlit orbit over the beaches of Southampton.

seen their old mounts. It is like watching them go back in time; standing a little straighter and looking a little younger when they are with the aircraft. We also see their children and grandchildren realize what a great roll their parents and grandparents had in the history of our country. Here on Long Island, building airplanes for the war was a big part of our heritage. We also meet people with awesome pride because their mother or father built the airplanes. Everyone had pride."

Bob and Chris love to tell stories about how sharing their airplanes touch people's lives; typically at airshows, but not always. Once while en-route to a flyover in Maryland, ATC handed them off to the tower at Dover Air Force Base. The tower asked if they would be willing to make a low pass. They obliged. Chris was flying lead in the Mustang and Bob was on his wing in the P-40 as the tower directed them down over a precise spot on the field. They flew the pass low and fast, then departed to the south. When they landed in Maryland, there was a phone call waiting from a Colonel at Dover AFB. Somewhat concerned they might have irritated the base commander, they decided to let things cool off before they returned the call. Monday morning Bob received this e-mail.

Almost the white sands of Normandy during the War, Bob crosses over the beach. The cockpit of the Warhawk is as pristine as the rest of the plane. Bob leads Chris back to Brookhaven as the sun sets.

of the men & women of the 180th Fighter Wing as well as Sonny's family and wife Lorin, I'd like to say thanks and wish you continued success with your fantastic organization.

Sincerely,

Operations Group Commander
Toledo F-16's OHANG

The quick thinking tower operator took the opportunity to make a meaningful addition to a sad ceremony.

It is stories like these that inspire Bob and Chris to fly and share these historic airplanes. "It is a way to show history", says Chris. "To show the public something they rarely get to see; to help keep history alive. It is an honor for us to be the caretakers of these great aircraft. "

Chris, born in 1980, is one of the younger pilots flying Mustangs today. That will make him 70 years old in 2050. When asked if he will be flying the Mustang then, he said, "I hope so! I'll be actively involved in the effort to keep them flying."

His dad reflected, "Not that long ago, I was changing his diapers. Now I am flying a few feet off his wing at 250 knots. What a thrill."

And what about the future of the Baranaskas Fighter Pilot Legacy? Fear not, It is destined to carry on into the long distant future, Chris and his lovely wife Jen recently gave birth to a beautiful baby boy, CJ and you should see his eyes light up whenever he is around the hanger.

Dear Fellow Warriors,

I would like to pass along a heartfelt "Thank You" to whoever flew across Dover around noon on June 23rd. All I could get was the callsign of N1RB and that it was a P-51 and P-40. We had dispatched a KC-135 from Ohio to come pick up the remains of our lost friend Lt Col Kevin "Sonny" Sonnenberg. He lost his life while piloting an F-16 over Iraq. The timing of your impromptu flyby just as they got his casket in the jet was perfect and Sonny would have been proud. On behalf

It is hard to find a more beautiful and peaceful back drop than the barrier beaches of Long Island in October. Opposite page shows Chris bearing down on the MachPOD remote camera as the Skymaster drags these two classic warbirds over the ocean at the end of a perfect Indian Summer Saturday.

FAGEN FIGHTERS

With a family connection dating back to the beaches of Normandy, it is no wonder that Ron Fagen has surrounded himself with the premier fighters of World War II.

The top frame on this page shows the crew after our B-25 photo mission in Granite Falls. Left to right is Greg Poe, Ron Fagen, Evan Fagen and Rob Ator. Bottom right is the restoration shop crew. Opposite page shows Ron watching as Kevin Eldridge flies the Heritage Flight mission in Duluth.

For Ron Fagen, aviation is as much an integral part of his personal life as his professional life. In his early years in Southwestern Minnesota, Ron's father owned and flew several taildragger aircraft using them often to advance customer relations in his livestock trucking company. At age 13, Ron learned to fly. Over the years Ron flew for recreation and slowly built a significant amount of flight hours. By 1985, he was flying a Pitts S1S in competition aerobatics, and it was during this time that Ron really began advancing his piloting skills as well as his appetite for higher performing aircraft.

By the early nineties, competition aerobatics had grown somewhat stale for Ron, who by now had significantly grown his industrial construction firm, Fagen, Inc. He set his sights on bigger things in aviation. Ron purchased his first P-51 Mustang from the estate of Jack Sandberg.

As he prepared to take delivery of the World War II treasure in 1994, Ron became one of the first "students" to complete Lee Lauderbacks' newly created Stallion 51 training curriculum down in Kissimmee, Florida. After the intensive ground school and twelve flight hours, he earned his L.O.A. or letter of authorization in the P-51 and soon after was flying his own Mustang from his home field in Granite Falls.

Once his courtship with the Mustang was

consummated, Ron fell head-long into warbirds first obtaining a P-40 Warhawk project which was finished using the markings of Shirley II, the mount of Granite Falls native Ray Callaway who flew in the famed Flying Tigers under Claire Chennault. The Shirley II received the Phoenix award at the EAA AirVenture Convention in Oshkosh, Wisconsin, in 1998. Several P-40 Warhawk projects followed. He formed a world-class restoration shop solely for the purpose of preserving these rare gems of history. In 2006, the Bengal Tiger P-40K that they restored first captured the coveted Grand Champion trophy at Oshkosh. Shortly thereafter, Ron acquired a P-38 from Stephen Grey in the UK and scored the Best World War II Fighter victory at Oshkosh with its presentation there as RUFF STUFF in 2007.

Ron has had a unique personal connection to the P-38 ever since he was a kid. During the Normandy invasion of World War II, his father Ray was pinned down on the beach by German defenses. At some point during the battle, Ray looked up and saw a flight of P-38 Lightning's rolling in to strafe the German positions. The pilots scored direct hits on the enemy emplacements and allowed the troops to advance ultimately to Berlin. Ever since hearing Ray's first-hand account of the Lightning in action, Ron has considered the P-38 the plane that saved his father's life.

The personal connection to aviation runs deep in

Opposite page shows the Fagen Fighters in trail formation with Rob Ator in the lead with the P-38. This page bottom shows Ron and Kevin just after the Heritage Flight mission in Duluth.

This page shows Evan Fagen in the P-51 formed up along side of the Pat Harker's B-25 Lady Luck. Opposite page shows Evan from the B-25 tail gunner position with Rob in trail.

334th

the Fagen family starting first with his father, but Ron has already begun passing the torch. Wife, Diane is a licensed pilot having hours logged with legend Duane Cole. Son, Aaron soloed in the family-owned SuperCub. Son Evan took his pilot skills to the next level at the controls of a Christen Eagle, a two seat aerobatic plane that allowed him to receive instruction from world famous aerobatic pilots Wayne Handley, Sean Tucker, Greg Poe, and John Morrisey. When the phenomenal 4-ship airshow team, the Northern Lights disbanded in 2003, Evan acquired one of their Extra 300L 2-seat monoplanes that he flies to this day when not at the controls of the Mustang.

With Evan flying the Mustang, and Ron happily at the controls of the Warhawk, it was up to Fagen, Inc. flight department manager, Rob Ator to man up the P-38. Rob has thousands of flight hours built mostly in corporate aircraft. Today, he is in charge of the company's multiple Cessna Citation

These pages show Ron Fagen in the P-40 flying with the B-25 as well as the exquisite details of this world class restoration.

jets, a B-58 Baron and an A-36 Bonanza.

These days, the P-38 is one of the few warbirds around the country certified to fly with the USAF Heritage Flight, an official Air Force program that matches up formations of vintage fighters with today's state-of-the-art front-line combat jets. These formations fly in front of millions of Americans each year at airshow venues around the country. Pilot Kevin Eldridge from Chino, California is most often the civilian Heritage pilot that gets to fly RUFF STUFF, but Steve Hinton is also qualified in Fagen's "fork-tailed devil."

Truly a field of dreams that emerges out the corn south of town, the Granite Falls airport is home to the Fagen Fighters and Fagen, Inc. flight department.

AIR COMBAT COMMAND HERITAGE FLIGHT

Like a sixty year old shadow that mirrors two tails and twin engines, the P-38 Lightning blazed the trail in aerial ground attack warfighting that is fullfilled today by the A-10 Thunderbolt.

Flash.... Thunder!

Essay by Paul "HARB" Brown
USAF A-10 West Demo Pilot

Forming up on Doug Rozendaal's Baron with the photo flawless A-10, "Harb" Brown leads Kevin Eldridge in Ron Fagen's P-38 over Lake Superior near Duluth, MN during the Monaco Air airshow in July.

Snort Snodgrass flies Jim Read's Mustang Excalibur in a 2-ship Saturday Heritage Flight at Oshkosh with the ACC F-22 Raptor.
Bottom left shows the Sunday Heritage Flight at Oshkosh with Steve Hinton in lead flying the P-38 Glacier Girl and the Raptor.

My name is Paul Brown and I'm a fighter pilot in the United States Air Force. In 2008 and 2009 I had the distinct honor to serve as the A-10 West Demonstration Pilot. The job is fantastic – I get to fly all over the country in a fighter burning someone else's gas! How can you top that? Here's how:

The United States Air Force Heritage Flight.

You see, I've been flying my whole life and I was raised into a family of pilots. I fly the A-10 for my day job and then escape to the local municipal airport whenever possible to fly my Cessna 180. That wonderful creation of Clyde Cessna has carried me from the gravel bars of the Yukon River with tundra tires, to the frozen surface of the Ruth Glacier on Mt. McKinley on skis, and to the southernmost reaches of Texas on wheels. I fly every chance I get. I live and breathe aviation. It's a lifestyle to my family. It's what we do; it's who we are. We're pilots.

That's why the Air Force Heritage Flight is so fantastic. Because I "get it." Look at the individuals and aircraft in the program. It's like a "who's who" issue of United States aviation history. Let me tell you, flying the single-ship demonstration profile is exhilarating, but nothing gets my adrenaline pumping like rejoining on the wing of a Skyraider, Warhawk, Thunderbolt, Mustang, Sabre, Lightning, or Phantom. Even the names themselves are legendary. Add the pilots inside those famous aircraft and the program becomes a childhood dream come true.

I will never forget my first Heritage Flight with Ed Shipley and Kevin Eldridge. They were flying a gorgeous TF-51 Mustang and Kevin was in the back seat for his upgrade as a Heritage Flight pilot. It was the first of

many training sorties during the 2008 Heritage Flight Conference at Davis-Monthan AFB, AZ. I couldn't believe how small the Mustang was compared to my A-10! When I was a child, the Mustang was a BIG fighter. It's amazing how time changes our perspectives. But one thing that hadn't changed was the sweet sound of a Rolls Royce Merlin. I was stunned to hear the Merlin IN my cockpit - through the canopy, helmet, and earplugs. The same thing happened the following day when I rejoined with Thomas "Gumby" Gregory III in Lone Star Flight Museum's P-47 "Tarheel Hal." What a dream to be flying with my fighter's namesake – the P-47 Thunderbolt and an A-10 Thunderbolt II. They were designed to accomplish the same mission, albeit it 40+ years apart! The rumbling of the P-47's Pratt & Whitney R-2800 penetrated all the way though my cockpit and into my ears. Talk about the sound of freedom! Each and every time I finish my aerobatic routine and rejoin the Heritage Flight I experience these same emotions. For the first few seconds, before my brain gets busy performing the routine, it's 1944 and it's real!

As if flying on the wing of these great pilots and warbirds isn't cool enough, how about flying IN them? Yet another occasional perk of the job! Ed Shipley fulfilled a life-long dream of mine by providing my Heritage Flight orientation sortie in Steven Hinton's P-51 "Wee Willy II." I must have made a dozen phone calls to friends and family on the taxi out to the runway. I had to let them hear the wonderful Merlin music and rub in that I was going to fly a Mustang! Woo hoo! I was literally in tears as we broke ground, sucked the gear up, and climbed away. The airplane flew as expected and handled very similar to modern day fighters. Upon landing, I couldn't stop grinning for hours. That is a flight I'll never forget. Now I just need to talk Ed into letting me fly from the front seat!

All of these pages show the various formation changes and ground shots I was able to capture of Harb Brown and Kevin Eldridge at the Monaco Air airshow in Duluth. Opposite top left is Kevin Eldridge manning up the P-38 owned by Ron Fagen.

Last year I had the privilege of flying with many different Heritage Flight pilots. Three of them I've mentioned previously, Ed Shipley, Kevin Eldridge, and Gumby Gregory. I also flew with Major General Bill Anders (USAF Reserve, ret.), his son Greg "BA" Anders, Capt Dale "Snort" Snodgrass (USN, ret.), Chuck Hall, Steve Hinton, Kevin Eldridge, Lee Lauderback, Vlado Lenoch, Brigadier General Regis Urschler (USAF, ret.), and Alan Henley. The only two I didn't fly with are Jimmy Beasley and Brad Hood. I hope our paths cross in 2009. If these names aren't familiar to you, I encourage you to look them up on the internet. But be prepared,

some of their stories are so amazing, they read stranger than fiction. I've spent hours upon hours reading their accomplishment and accolades.

The pictures on the following pages were shot at the Duluth Airshow 2008. Kevin Eldridge was flying Ron Fagen's P-38 "Ruff Stuff." Here are the details: I had worked for weeks getting Air Combat Command's approval for a photo shoot and was successful! Now the weather and airplanes had to cooperate. The initial plan was to have Erik Hildebrandt shoot from a B-25 but the Mitchell was at another show that weekend. We improvised and Doug Rozendaal ended up flying a Beech Baron for the

shoot. My safety officer, Captain Sean Baerman, flew right seat and Erik directed the formations.

As luck would have it, the weather was downright terrible the day of the shoot. The forecast wasn't supposed to get any better than 800 foot overcast and the show producers were very disappointed. We waited around for hours to see if the forecaster was wrong and then in an instant, a hole appeared. Then another! We just might be able to pull this thing off! Since the P-38 wasn't IFR equipped we asked the tower for a special VFR departure to get out of controlled airspace and on top of the clouds.

We were granted the clearance and soon launched into the wild blue yonder for a rejoin over Lake Superior. Kevin formed up shortly thereafter and the fun began. I kept thinking, "How cool is this? Two twin-tailed, twin-engine fighters from two very different wars." All too soon Erik had taken hundreds of pictures and it was time to land. Kevin and I serviced our planes and got ready for the afternoon air show performance.

I was stunned when we viewed the fruits of our labor. Everyone thinks they're paintings or have been "Photoshopped." I can assure you, they are neither. On behalf of the A-10 West Demonstration Team, the USAF Heritage Flight, Kevin Eldridge, Ron Fagen, Doug Rozendaal, and Erik Hildebrandt, we hope you enjoy these photos about 1/10th as much as we enjoyed making them!

Blue skies and tailwinds,
-Paul "Harb" Brown

ACC A-10 West Demo Team. Left to right: SSgt Bobby Williams, Capt Sean "Ole'" Baerman, Capt Paul "Harb" Brown, SrA Kent Sedgwick, SrA Joshua Ames and A1C Thomas Cannon.

JACQUIE B AIRSHOWS

In an industry largely populated with brash male egos and cut-throat aerial maneuvering, Jacquie B offers airshow crowds a softer side of adrenaline. Smooth and approachable, her presence on the flight line is the perfect antidote to all the testosterone.

Essay By Estelle Brown
SkyHighPub@verizon.net

Jacquie gives an interview to the local television crew at the Salinas International airshow. The front office of her Pitts shows the high-tech edge of this classic design.
Opposite page shows Jacquie blowing an "air-kiss" to Steve as she get's ready to strap on the airplane.

The odds were against Jacquie B to make it in the airshow world. She got a very late start in an exclusive industry that favors young men over older women, and this is what makes Jacquie's story so compelling.

Jacquie was 50 years young in 2003 when she flew her first airshow at Paraiso Winery in California, soaring way beyond the industry's invisible glass ceiling. She's the first female in airshow history to enter the business at that 'advanced' age, a credit to her persistence toward perfection, her powerful personality, and the confidence she had earned as an aerobatics student of Wayne Handley.

Jacquie reached a new level of success when she performed at the 28th California International Air Show in 2008. Only the most respected and time-tested pilots are asked to perform at the Salinas show. Finally-- after five years of 'probation' in which other emerging performers lose heart and drop away -- inclusion on the Salinas line-up signaled to Jacquie the industry's respect for her as a lead performer. The years of proving her position and finding her place in the pack was finally paying off.

It was also a full-circle milestone for Jacquie. "The Salinas air boss, Gale Rawitzer, was my first air boss at the Paraiso Winery show in 2003, so he had seen me from the beginning and had air bossed me at many shows leading up to Salinas. So, due in no small part to Gale singing my praises, I got to fly the 'big time' in California. Having Salinas on my resume now tells others that I've made their grade...."

Jacquie storms the skies with her single seat, 1986 Red Eagle Pitts S-1T biplane... one of only three aircraft built by Curtis Pitts to fly the airshow around the Statue of Liberty in

celebration of its completed refurbishment. Jacquie performs her 12-minute routine of hard-core tumbling maneuvers in her distinctive red, white and blue Pitts emblazoned with a powerful eagle's head.

Although her childhood dream to fly remained a lifelong passion, Jacquie didn't even start flight lessons until the age of 32. As the youngest of four children, Jacquie was inspired by her father, a private pilot and powerplant technical advisor for Douglas Aircraft. In fact, Jacquie attended her first airshow with her dad when she was just six weeks old. But Jacquie's love of flight didn't launch her into an aviation career for quite a while. Life got in the way.

In fact, Jacquie is a virtual Jill of All Trades, starting at entry level in several careers, then working her way up to executive status before moving on. A condensed retrospective works like a rapid-frame slide show: waitress, bartender, Estee Lauder cosmetics sales rep, assistant buyer, then buyer. Jacquie started ground school while working at Nordstrom in the Pacific Northwest.

Jacquie trained in a Cessna 150 at Felts Field in Spokane. She became a regular fence hanger there, and was soon invited by her new pilot friends to ride in all manner of aircraft. But one ride in a Pitts S-2B stood apart from all the others. After a flurry of loops and rolls, upside down and downside up, Jacquie was hooked for life.

She had always sensed, "There must be more to flying than just sitting in the cockpit, doing nothing while the plane goes straight ahead." Jacquie had finally discovered how she wanted to spend her time between take-offs and landings.

Flying orbits over the Golden Gate to get these sorts of images never gets old. This page shows Jacquie as she prepares to go wild for the crowd at the Salinas show.

Jacquie moved on to Seattle, working as a secretary and ski instructor, then in the parts department at Flightcraft, Inc. The company eventually promoted Jacquie to work at the Portland office as assistant to the president. Meanwhile, Jacquie continued flight lessons and skydiving. She finished her private pilot program in June 1986... and started a new dreaming process.

In 1995, the California sunshine called Jacquie to a law firm in San Francisco, where she managed a staff of 150 personnel. Her dream to train for competition aerobatics eventually materialized with retired airshow great Wayne Handley as her coach.

Jacquie had been flying a Pitts S-2B since 1997 in Livermore, California. She entered the International Aerobatic Club-sanctioned competition in August 2000 and rapidly reached

Jacquie B goes vertical and then pretends to make hit fellow performer Kent Pietsch in his Jelly Belly Interstate. Opposite page: the lady speaks for herself.

the Advanced category. Jacquie enjoyed four years of award-winning competition.

Jacquie learned quickly how to make it in the male-dominated industry. "I simply had to be good at whatever I did. Then the guys treated me as an equal."

While racing at Reno, Jacquie met Aeroshell Aerobatic Team's Gene McNeely, and they became great friends. The team helped her over the years with introductions and recommendations to show organizers.

"The Red Barons were also instrumental in my little successes. They took me under their wings and treated me like one of the team. I was one lucky girl at the start of it all to have such friends."

But there was more to learn about flying a Pitts than competition aerobatics offered, like tumbling the airplane. So Wayne started coaching Jacquie in basic air show maneuvers. One thing led to the other.

2003 marked the 100th anniversary of powered flight, Jacquie's 50th birthday, and her first airshow performance. That was the year Jacquie quit her regular job as a legal assistant, and became a full-time airshow professional.

"My success in this business is credited to Wayne Handley," Jacquie says. "If he hadn't asked me to fly Paraiso, I wouldn't be here today. I always wanted to learn something new, so it was only a matter of time that he should teach me to tumble an airplane. I loved it so much, that's all I wanted to do."

Looking forward to her sixth season in 2009, Jacquie has earned a reputation as a serious airshow performer. She has invested her total focus, energy and budget to becoming a success. Jacquie pays unusual attention to detail on the ground as well as in the sky. She strives to be a low-maintenance player who comes prepared, and is dependable, punctual, and pleasant.

Jacquie aims to make the best of imperfect situations, which are more the rule than the exception. "Nobody wants surprises, especially not at showtime, so I do what I say I will do, and then do whatever else I can do to make their show better," Jacquie says.

The result has been a list of achievements including flying more than 55 airshows from coast to coast, entertaining more than two million fans. Jacquie has logged more than 2,000 accident-free hours over her 23 years of flight, in aircraft ranging from a Stearman, an A-T6, T-28, Beechcraft King Air, Baron & Bonanza, Aeronca Champ, Citabria, Decathlon, Lancair, Sukhoi, Yak 52 and

and swim with her husband, David, and his two teen-age daughters.

Jacquie also speaks to various groups, motivating Girl Scout troops, public school groups, civic organizations, SWAN, Ninety-Nines and Women in Aviation gatherings.

Jacquie likes to say that the sky never runs out of up. Neither does Jacquie. She's a powerhouse of energy, plans and ideas. She never tires of flying, nor of exploring new ways to infect others with her passion. "We weren't born with wings, but I've learned that was just a temporary setback. I fly so others will dream and join me!"

"The most important thing to do in life is to make sure we teach others what we know, and share the love of flight with those who will take our places in the future," she says. "We must provide opportunity to those with the desire. Many young people will come along the way I did, paying for flight lessons one hour at a time. And yes, some will have their 'ticket' at 17. The ones who need help should never have trouble finding it."

True to character, Jacquie dedicates post-performance time to her fans, who line up for her autograph or have their pictures taken with her. Young girls are especially eager to meet the aviatrix.

"I'm a pilot first, but when young girls see what I'm doing, then get to talk to me and get an autograph, maybe they'll decide to dream a little bigger. If that happens, I've done a good job. I guess at my age, I'm the poster 'child' for anything is possible!"

Extra 300. In addition to her unrestricted, Level One ACE card, Jacquie holds a seaplane rating and a Commercial certificate in land-based aircraft.

Now Jacquie is 55. The full time airshow performer flies 15 shows per season, and averages 175 annual flight hours. She still finds time to play golf and tennis, water and snow ski, skeet shoot, ride motorcycles, run, lift weights, camp

pposite page shows the family hanger in Livermore in a photo taken by Estelle Brown. Top this page captures another precious part of the Jacquie B's job, connecting with the kids.

GREG POE
FAGEN INC

With unparalleled commitment and determination, Greg Poe demonstrates his passion for flight while inspiring America's youth to follow their dreams with his personal message of hope and purpose.

Dawn patrol over the Statue of Liberty is a great way to start the day. Dax piloted the A-36 all around NY Harbor at 1000 feet passing lower Manhattan, Brooklyn and the Varanzano Bridge. As a native New Yorker it was very cool.

Dax Wanless is a consummate professional and accomplished pilot in his own right. Seen on the top, he watches as Greg warms up the MX2 prior to his Oshkosh demo flight. Opposite page show Dax leading Greg in the A-36 Bonanza and is taken from Pat Harker's B-25 Lucky Lady flown by Pat and Jeff Hall over the corn fields near Fagen's Granite Falls base of operations.

For the past sixteen years, Greg Poe has become a mainstay on the national airshow circuit. Whether at the controls of Pitts Specials or Edge 540's, the Stearman biplane or his current mount, the Fagen MX2, he never fails to deliver one of the most original, hard charging and entertaining flight demonstrations at dozens of airshow events each year.

From America's heartland locations such as Omaha, Oshkosh or Indianapolis to far reaching locations like Puerto Rico, Alaska, Venezuela and Hawaii, Greg's passion for flight and desire to give it his all, is translated directly to millions of airshow fans across the globe.

"I realize the opportunity I've been given to do this is nothing less than a gift, and I don't intend to take it for granted" Says Greg.

That may be a bit of an understatement. Greg Poe Airshows and his corporate sponsor, Fagen Inc., have established themselves as one of the most sought-after acts in the airshow entertainment industry because of their commitment to deliver nothing less than the best. Fagen Inc., the largest design/builder of ethanol refineries in the nation as well as a major player in wind power generation and power plant construction have sponsored Poe at airshows around the country since 2006.

Greg was introduced to the Fagens by airshow legend Wayne Handley. Once the deal was struck between them, Greg ordered a new custom-built MX2, and purchased an A-36 Bonanza support plane for media and VIP rides. Fagens added two 24ft. support trailers and trucks (one for the eastern part of the U.S. and the other for the west).

Dale Wolin, a retired engineer from Hewlett Packard and experienced pilot was hired to drive the trucks and add on-site support. Debbie Seagle whose resume includes many years of experience in airshow marketing and advertising at the N'awlins and Cherry Point airshows, helps with public relations and media scheduling.

The first person Poe recruited to build his new team, however, is the one he calls the backbone of the entire operation - Dax Wanless. Wanless brings sixteen years of experience as an aircraft mechanic and FAA-designated aircraft inspector. He is a commercial pilot with an instrument rating and flies the Bonanza and the MX2 when needed.

The most visible contribution Dax provides to the operation (aside from being the voice of Greg Poe Airshows - he announces as Greg performs) is flying the Bonanza in close formation with Greg in the MX2. Reporters, photographers and Fagen VIP guests get a close-up and personal view of one of

Greg arcs over lower Manhattan as the morning haze slowly lifts behind the Brooklyn Bridge. Above top shows Greg's wing-mounted fish-eye lens as he orbits Lady Liberty and Ellis Island. The bottom shot shows Greg flying inverted down the runway during an actual performance at the Ft. Worth Alliance Airshow

the top aerobatic airplanes put through its paces at the hands of a world-class pilot. Add to that some of the most spectacular scenic backdrops from coast to coast and the results are breathtaking.

From the moment the team arrives at an airshow they set to work preparing for what Greg calls "game day." Preparation days are usually sun up to sun down, consisting of media and VIP flights, aerobatic practice flights, briefings, workouts and support trailer staging and set up. All designed to entertain throngs of people while educating them about the value and need for alternative fuel. After all, Greg is the only pilot in the world currently performing unlimited low-level aerobatics in an airplane powered with ethanol fuel. "We run 85 to 95 percent ethanol with a small amount of 100LL aviation fuel blend" says Dax. "The engine runs cooler and we get more horsepower."

"I still pinch myself sometimes," says Greg. "It's been a long road for a kid from Idaho who used to dream of flying, to actually get to live out his dreams."

A long road indeed! Poe grew up in Boise Idaho where he always seemed to be on the go and involved in activities. He was selected as the athlete of the year at his jr. high school, placed 2nd in a national collegiate speech competition and was chosen

as the student commencement speaker when he graduated from Boise State University. His aviation bug has its roots in the space program of the sixties but he didn't get a chance to actually fly until he was sixteen years old when family friend Walt Mousseau lit that fire with a short flight in a Cessna 150. The die was cast. Greg spent two years saving money from part time jobs and earned his pilots license at age nineteen. From there his flying career literally "took off."

After cutting his teeth flying the rugged Idaho backcountry, Greg attended the Reno Air Races and was hooked. He later earned his commercial, instrument and flight instructor ratings. But it was the basic aerobatic instruction drilled into him by his original flight instructor, John Chambers, that

Greg credits with really getting him started on his way to becoming a full time airshow pilot. And what a career it's been.

With over 8000 flight hours Greg has flown over 100 different types of airplanes in the last 34 years. Along the way he added multi-engine and floatplane ratings. Greg considers one of the highlights of his career to be the time he spent as the production test pilot for Aviat Aircraft in Afton, Wyoming.

During that time he was responsible to complete the FAA required test flights for all Pitts and Husky aircraft that rolled out the factory doors.

He's been at the controls of a WWII B-17 bomber, acquired an LOA in the British Hawker Hunter jet, and received incentive rides in the F-15 and F-16 fighter jets as well as riding along with the U.S. Navy Blue Angels during one of their airshow performances. He has been selected to compete in several

After we flew the New York Harbor mission from the Atlantic City airshow, we decided it was so cool we tried it again the next day. This time, the air was crystal clear with unlimited visibility. Opposite shows Greg in a knife-edge behind Dax in the Bonanza.

televised airshow competitions placing 2nd in the World Freestyle Sportflying championships in 1999, and 3rd in the World Aerobatic Federation championships in 2000.

Greg has been featured in programs such as Modern Marvels, Ripley's Believe it or Not as well as programs on CBS, ESPN, Fox Sports and the Discovery channel.

Greg and his family suffered a life-altering loss in 2002 with the drug-related death of their son Ryan. In an effort to create something positive out of such a tragedy, Greg established the Ryan J. Poe Foundation to support a program he named "Elevate Your Life."

"We typically go into a community a few days before an airshow and visit schools to present Elevate Your Life," Greg says. It's a positive program that encourages young people to believe in themselves and tap into their natural talent to create success in their lives. "It's very rewarding when you can use what you do for a living and are so passionate about, to help inspire young people to follow their dreams." Greg has given over one hundred different presentations around the country and doesn't see it slowing down. "The older I get the more I realize the opportunity we all have to be a positive influence in people's lives.

The future of Greg Poe Airshows and Elevate Your Life is poised for continued growth, utilizing aviation as a means of educating the public about the importance of alternative "green energy" and encouraging America's youth to follow their dreams. As Greg likes to tell those who attend his presentations, "Always aim for the sky."

ELEVATE YOUR LIFE
powered by dream
Greg Poe AIR SHOWS

Opposite top frame is yet another B-25 tail shot that shows Greg leading the Fagen Fighters. Below that is Greg over Ellis Island in NY Harbor where I went with my dad as a teenager in his high school history class field trip. It is an amazing place. Next to that is Greg signing autographs for school kids following his inspiring Elevate Your Life presentation.

Greg leads the Fagen Fighters on an early morning B-25 photo mission over the corn fields near Granite Falls, MN. Opposite is a final turn in front of the Brooklyn Bridge before we headed back down to Atlantic City after this epic dawn patrol to NYC.

MICHAEL GOULIAN

From Tiger Woods and Warren Buffett to Michael Jordan and Bill Gates, top performers in every field have this in common: meticulous planning, exhaustive preparation and flawless execution.

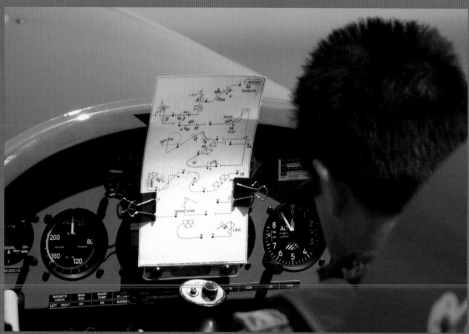

The Aresti card of aerobatic notations describes with symbols what Michael's routine looks like on paper. The powerful Lycoming Thunderbolt IO-580 easily pulls the new Extra 300SHP through knife-edge passes and will surely advance Michael in the Red Bull Air Races the next season. Previous page and opposite as seen from the Skymaster at Oshkosh.

After more than two decades of aerobatic flying, Michael Goulian has used that same formula to ascend to the highest levels of his field.

To reach this level and stay there, Goulian lives his life in perpetual motion, feeding off the energy of his fans and the crowds that come to watch him fly. With a global performance schedule that would exhaust most professional athletes, Goulian performs and competes in dozens of cities on five different continents in a season that spans from February to November. He flies perhaps the most aggressive, yet perfectly conducted high performance aerobatic demonstrations in the world. When Michael is flying, he has a style that clearly separates him from his peers and captivates the fans with an emotionally charged show.

From the start, Goulian has been focused on precision. At age 22, he became the youngest aerobatic champion in U.S. history by winning the US Advanced National Aerobatic Championship in 1990. Just five years later, he reached the pinnacle of U.S. aerobatic achievement when he was

crowned National Aerobatic Champion in the elite Unlimited Category.

By the late 1990s, Goulian redirected his considerable energy and talents to the unique challenges of air show display flying. With meticulous planning, tireless preparation and precise execution, Goulian was quickly recognized as one of the most entertaining and professional pilots in the business. In 2006, in recognition that Goulian had reached the very highest level in his profession, the air show industry bestowed its premier honor on Michael when he was awarded the coveted Art Scholl Memorial Award for Showmanship.

The physical demands of performing aerobatics at the highest levels require intense strength, focus and commitment in an environment that is far less forgiving than most sports. For Goulian, it is precisely that requirement that he always be at the top of his game – mentally and physically -- that focuses his attention on the challenges he faces every time he straps in to perform at air shows or compete in air races. This commitment to excellence has also helped

outside of the cockpit. He is the author of two instructional aerobatic books and enjoys a well-deserved reputation as a passionate advocate for general aviation as an accomplished speaker.

A natural optimist and self-admitted perfectionist, Goulian exudes an aura of positive professionalism that infects everyone around him. From his ground

The increased roll rate of the Extra 300SHP is obvious in the sequence above. Opposite shows the big-bore Lycoming Thunderbolt engine up close and growling smoothly.

crew and teammates to his wife and business partner Karin, Goulian Aerosports is an organizational extension of Michael Goulian himself. Indeed, by any objective measure, the company is the top-performing organization in the entire air sports industry. Goulian's successful air show operation is now complemented by his participation in the immensely popular Red Bull Air Races, a worldwide aviation competition and television spectacle that is seen by more than 400 million people annually.

Like the highly competitive athletes in other fields that he emulates, Goulian is not content to simply be the best. He is constantly challenging himself and his organization to continuously improve and excel. Whether competing in the Red Bull Air Race World Championship, fine-

tuning some aspect of his air show display, or securing additional exposure for his corporate sponsors, Goulian is not satisfied when he achieves the goals others have set for him. He measures his performance by another standard: the considerably more difficult goals that he has established for himself.

During the EAA Convention at Oshkosh and throughout the year for that matter, Michael relies heavily on his co-crew chiefs Mike Cappiello and Marcy Gruener both for ferrying the Extra and keeping her spotless and running smoothly..

SENNHEISER
aviation headsets

Castrol Avi

Michael Goulian

Sky Dynamics Corporation   Airflow Performance, Inc.

The EXTRA 300SHP could provide Michael the maneuverability edge and the increased speed he needs to attain victory in the RED BULL AIR RACES this coming season.

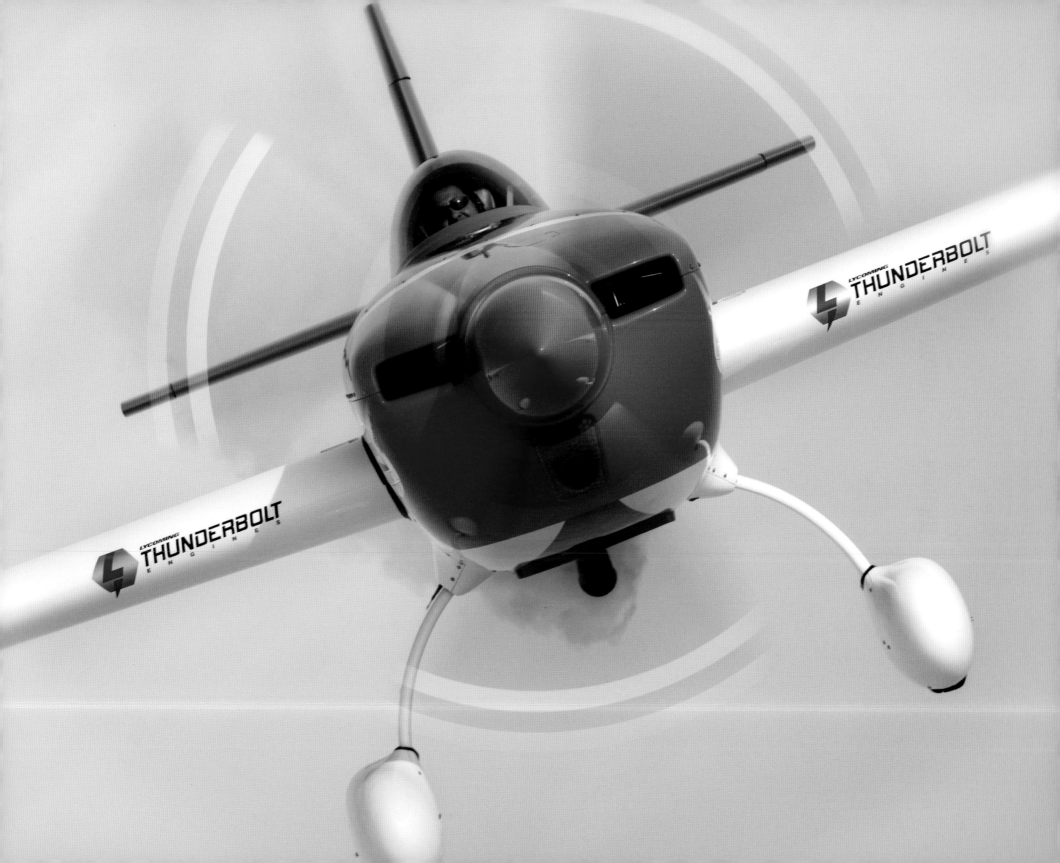

PATTY WAGSTAFF
CIRRUS DESIGN

Patty lives by the motto, the harder you train, the luckier you get. Her professional success and perfect safety record prove it.

Essay By Estelle Brown
SkyHighPub@verizon.net

CIRRUS

Patty flashes a "peace- sign" which these days seems to have renewed significance. Watching on at Oshkosh as she prepares for her spectacular solo performance in front of tens of thousands of aviation pilgrims. Above right is a departure shot that Jeff Green took from the ground at Sun n Fun as we left to make the air-to-air images in this chapter.

Patty Wagstaff is an airshow superstar, achieving record-breaking status in both aerobatic competition and performance. This leading lady of airshows is respected and emulated for her surpassing skill, precision, discipline and beauty, both in flight and as a person.

Patty lives by the motto, the harder you train, the luckier you get. Her professional success and perfect safety record prove it.

Flying a world-renowned low-level aerobatic routine before millions of spectators annually, Patty's breathtaking performances demonstrate the precision and complexity of modern, unlimited hard-core aerobatics. Her aggressive, yet smooth style sets the standard for performers worldwide.

A six-time member of the U.S. Aerobatic Team, Patty has won the gold, silver and bronze medals in Olympic-level international aerobatic competition. She is the first woman to be named U.S. National Aerobatic champion... and one of the few pilots to win the title three times.

A lifelong curiosity led Patty to attend her first airshow in British Columbia in 1983. "I can do that!" she thought. By 1985 -- five years after gaining her private pilot's license -- Patty earned a spot on the U.S. Aerobatic Team.

Patty's "luck" is actually skill, developed from years of focused training. As a result, Patty has captured the most prestigious and coveted aviation/aerobatics awards the industries offer. To enumerate each distinctive honor would consume a third of the text in this chapter. For a complete listing, see www.pattywagstaff.com .

Here's a sampling: Patty is a six-time recipient of the 'First Lady of Aerobatics' Betty Skelton Award and has been inducted into the National Aviation Hall of Fame. She has received the International Council of Air Shows Sword of Excellence and the Bill Barber Award for Showmanship. Recently, she accepted the Lifetime Achievement Award from the Air Force Association, was inducted into the EAA/IAC Hall of Fame, and received the NAA/99's Katherine Wright Award.

To Patty, the sky represents adventure, freedom and challenge. Growing up the daughter a Japan Airlines captain, Patty was only 10 when her father let her take the controls of his DC-6, and she was smitten with the lifelong desire to fly.

While living in Alaska, Patty learned to fly in a Cessna 185 floatplane. She went on to earn her Commercial, Instrument, Seaplane and Commercial Helicopter Ratings. She is a Flight and Instrument Instructor, rated and qualified to fly several airplanes, including World War II warbirds and jets.

To observers, Patty Wagstaff has already accumulated a lifetime of achievements, opportunities and adventures. Among them are having one of her airplanes on display in the Smithsonian National Air & Space Museum in Washington D.C., exhibited next to Amelia Earhart's Lockheed Vega. Patty has trained with the Russian Aerobatic Team and has flown in exotic locales like South America, Russia, Europe, Mexico and Iceland. She is a member of the Screen Actors Guild, Motion Picture Pilots Association, and United Stuntwomen's Association, working as a stunt pilot and aerial coordinator for the film and television industries.

Patty has been Hawker Beechcraft's demo pilot for their turboprop military trainer, the Texan II, at international airshows since 1999. Patty also spends her off seasons giving recurrency training to bush pilots of the Kenya Wildlife Service in Africa, who patrol for poachers. Not to mention Patty's other interests, including competing in horse show jumping competitions, riding her motorcycle and bicycle, and renovating her 1926 Spanish Revival home in St. Augustine, Florida.

Evidently, Patty is not ready to slow down... not by any means. "I don't feel that I've reached the limit of my potential," says Patty. "There is more to learn about flying, and I'm still enjoying it. I'm not ready to retire. I'm too young! I have too much energy! Besides, the best people in the world are in aviation. Why should I quit?"

The future is full of possibilities, as Patty sees it. "I keep myself open to opportunities and stay involved in everything to see what the next dimension will be. Eventually, my path defines itself and

then I understand which elements brought me there. Meanwhile, I need to be authentic to what I'm supposed to be doing."

Fans, peers and industry experts alike recognize the vital role Patty plays as ambassador for aviation in general and for airshows in particular. So it's not surprising that innovative aircraft manufacturer Cirrus Design wooed Patty to become their sponsored airshow performer. Now she's their most ardent spokesperson.

"Previously, I had owned a couple of B-55 Barons," Patty explains. "I thought of myself as a Beechcraft person and didn't see the need to switch."

"But once I finally got into a Cirrus, I thought, "This is beautiful! I want one!""

This page shows the crystal clear skies of Oshkosh in July. Opposite shows Patty's crew chief Phil Geraci as he returns from running the ribbon cut when Patty's lucky few get to hold her poles.

Patty got her wish. Her single-seat composite aerobatic steed -- the Extra 300S -- combines superb quality, impeccable engineering, and maximum performance (exceeding most fighter aircraft) to consistently perform according to Patty's world-class demands.

Cirrus manufactures the composite SR-22 GTS, the world's best selling airplane that Patty flies as her support airplane to and from airshows. She loves the comfort, beauty and performance of the aircraft.

"The airplane is so well designed and it does not have an industrial feel like some of the other light aircraft. There is a comfortable room flow to the interior and the gorgeous, intuitive panel is all glass. They've gone out of their way to incorporate every extra safety feature available from impact-resistant seats to the AmSafe airbag-equipped shoulder harnesses. How could a pilot not appreciate the thought that went into the design of this airplane?"

Patty feels that Cirrus' message exemplifies her own mission: focusing on the art of flying and the importance of exposing aviation to people through airshows.

"The ability to fly an airplane gave me the confidence, self esteem and sense of accomplishment I otherwise would not have had," Patty says. She is passionate about sharing that power of discovery and achievement with anyone dreaming of becoming a pilot.

"I've met prospective pilots who face obstacles that threaten to

discourage them from pursuing their goal. Aviation is sometimes perceived as being beyond their skill level or means. Both Cirrus and I want to impart the message that flying is a possibility for more people. Flying can open your world and make it smaller at the same time. It's always worthwhile as a means to enhance your lifestyle, but it's also about beauty, freedom and an elevated perspective. I want ordinary people to realize it is within their reach to be up in the sky like I am, flying at 180-200 miles an hour!"

Patty says she didn't set out to become a role model. "I just wanted to fly airplanes. But now I feel it's my responsibility, because it's within my power to help someone out. If a small act of kindness on my part makes all the difference to someone else, I am rewarded. I can give of myself because so much has been given to me."

Seen here with "Cirrus OnStar" a horse she competed in show jumping, Patty is almost as passionate about riding as he is about her aerial performances.
Horse photos by Jeff Berlin.

All of the air-to-air images in this chapter were made on a single mission at Sun n Fun in Florida with Doug Rozendaal at the controls of my Skymaster.

THE COLLABORATORS

The unassuming name belies the energy and significance of this remarkable 4-ship aerobatic quartet that makes music with the wind at 200 miles an hour.

Essay By Estelle Brown

Ideally set up for flying VIPs in their multi-seat aircraft after their rigorous demonstrations, the Collaborators are true ambassadors of aviation all around the country.

"It's kind of a dumb name, until you really think about it. I can't even remember who came up with it, but we all agreed it was perfect. We've got to work together seamlessly as a team to pull this off. The Collaborators just kind of stuck."

That's the venerable Sean D. Tucker, talking about his latest claim to fame and dream-come-true: the four-ship civilian aerobatic formation team he introduced in 2007 with Bill Stein, Ben Freelove and Eric Tucker.

The Collaborators debut has infused a fresh shot of adrenaline onto the air show stage. Featuring four very different pilot personalities flying four disparate high performance aerobatic airplanes, The Collaborators have brought a new brand of big-sky, energetic artistry to the scene.

Their 14-minute show draws together power and grace, elegance and chaos. With innovative close-formation maneuvers like the echelon, diamond, arrowhead, half Cuban and the inside-out-eight, spectators are awestruck by the graceful choreography of each difficult configuration. The

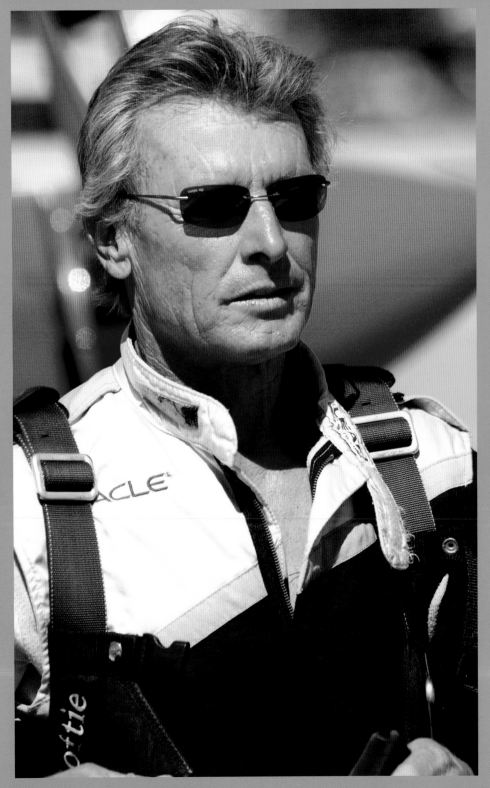

Collaborators are the only team in the U.S. to execute the demanding three-quarter outside loop. The Melee shakes fans from their dream-state, building the show to a crescendo as all four planes cut through the aerobatic box simultaneously, in a series of apparent near-miss dives at 250 miles an hour. Then the climactic Finale features a four-ship rejoin in a swooping diamond that ends with a dynamic bomb-burst.

The Collaborators consist of Sean as the Lead in his Challenger Biplane; Ben as Right Wing in his Extra 300L; Eric as Left Wingman in his Extra 300L; and Bill as Slot Pilot with his Edge 540.

Ben is the director of operations and aerobatic instructor at Sean's Tutima Academy of Aviation Safety. He is also a serious aerobatic competitor, flying in the Advanced category. He has logged more than 3,000 hours in more than 40 different types of aircraft. On the side, Ben is a professional musician, specializing in jazz and rhythm & blues bass. But primarily, Sean considers Ben a serious purist as a student of aerobatics, who chooses a "hermit-like

Like the big brother on the team, Bill Stein is a calm and steady figure for both the young pilots as well as the frenetic Sean D. In the air however, Bill tears it up like the little kid at heart that he is.

Always looking to try something new and push the envelope, Sean cranks the Challenger into a series of falling tumbles as the pure speed blurs across my camera frame.

existence in order to fulfill his dream of being a top aerobatic pilot."

Eric is Sean's equally-dynamic son who has had to earn his place in the industry, because Sean actually dissuaded him from pursuing an aerobatic career. "I didn't want Eric to get into this hard, dangerous business," Sean admits. "But he has earned the right. He graduated from college with honors in aerospace aeronautics and became a test pilot in his own right. With Eric's work ethic and business acumen, he has become a great asset as a Tutima flight instructor and a Collaborators team member." Eric

gained formation experience in 2005 as a member of the Stars of Tomorrow flight demo team.

Bill is not only the slot pilot for The Collaborators, but the team's safety officer, as well. He is also a formation specialist and aerobatic instructor at the Tutima Academy. Bill is a former Red Baron Stearman Squadron pilot with extensive experience in aerobatic competition and coaching. He also has enjoyed a 22-year Silicon Valley career, including a most recent post as vice president of engineering for HotJobs. com. Not surprisingly, Sean describes Bill as "intellectually sharp, and I hold utmost respect for him. Without Bill's expertise, and his commitment to safety and excellence, The Collaborators would be nowhere as dynamic as we've become."

"It's a challenge to fuse dissimilar planes and personalities, but we're all on the same page, shooting for that same brass ring on the merry-go-round. As long as we make good art in the sky and

Eric Tucker brings his own flair and flavor to the circuit. While firmly connected by his blood ties to the industry, Eric contributes a fresh approach to both the flying and the business aspects of airshows.

Ben Freelove is the precise, by-the-numbers player of the bunch. An accomplish aerobatic instructor at Sean's Tutima Academy in King City, CA, Ben moonlights with the Collaborators whenever the team hits the road during the season.

inspire people, leaving an impression of reverence in them for the air show... we're a success."

Not to say they're satisfied. The Collaborators continue to critique and refine their artistry and execution, reaching for that elusive perfect flight. They practiced 500 times for six shows in 2008, working out their mission: to elevate the art of the airshow experience to the next level. Every flight is one more chance to strive for perfection.

Sean likes to think of the formation team as a paintbrush making elegant, broad strokes through the sky. "We're just really lucky to have this perfect storm of talent, dreams and passion working together as The Collaborators," he says. "I'm blessed to work with each one of these guys, who share my dream and pursue it with sacrifice, hard work and the goal of perfection. The Collaborators used to just be a dream.

Now it's reality!"

"Like father-like son" is a cliche' that just seems to work when you look at these two amazing pilots fly in the same airspace. All dads should be so lucky and proud.

RAF RED ARROWS OVER QUONSET POINT

On the final stop of a very rare North American tour, the Red Arrows dazzle New England and load up with bar-b-que grills to take back across the Pond to live like Yanks.

A bit less formal than the Blues or the Thunderbirds, the Red Arrows performance is rooted in much larger formations and a comic narration worthy of this FAMILY GUY crowd. Mini-boss Kyle Gurnon yucks is up with Red Arrow narrator "Flight Lieutenant Andy Robins.

REDS 123

REDS 125

126 FRC4 Wing Commander Larry Gallogally is flanked by his daughter Caroline for the Red Arrow Finale at show center of the Rhode Island National Guard airshow at Quonset Point, RI.

REDS 127

RI ARMY NATIONAL GUARD COMES HOME

After over one year deployed to a non-disclosed location in Iraq, the 169th Military Police Company of the Rhode Island Army National Guard get a well-earned hero's welcome home. Thank you troopers for your ongoing service!!

WELCOME HOME
SPC. ROBERT BESTWICK!
RHODE ISLAND 169th
MILITARY POLICE COMPANY

Instead of taking Greyhound buses back from their rotator flight arrival in Virginia, the 143rd AW co-located at Quonset flew two C-130J cargo planes down to bring the troops the rest of the way home in time for the airshow/open house. Well done!

US NAVY STRIKE-FIGHTER DEMO/ LEGACY FLIGHT

On the eve of the Centennial of Naval Aviation, the US Navy has a lot to celebrate. For nearly 100 years, carrier aviation has been the backbone of this nation's global influence.

Essay by David C. Nilsen

VFA-122 Lead : CO/CDR Greg "HYFI" Harris / LT Todd "Fokker" Royles Dash-2- LT Mike "Tina" Turner / HM2 Thomas Lochowicz
Dash-3- LT Brad "FID" Garms / LT Patrick "Pigpen" Bernhard Dash-4- LT Damon "Profile" Loveless / LT Darin "Baghak" Dean

Sitting on the open ramp of a C-130J is about the only way you can make images like these. With my very best friends from the 143AW in Rhode Island, we lead this division formation of Super Hornets up the coast from Salinas, over the Golden Gate, past downtown SF and back out to the Pacific. It was an incredible opportunity for all of us and we are proud to have been able to bring back these pictures to share with everyone. Toward the end of the flight, we were joined by Chuck Wentorth in the Legacy program F-4U Corsair based in Paso Robles, CA.

Strike Fighters, the F/A-18 Hornet and Super Hornet family, are the tip of the Naval Aviation spear. "Legacy" Hornets, F/A-18 A through D, have been with the fleet since 1980. Super Hornets, F/A-18Es and Fs, better known around the carriers as "Rhinos," have been with the fleet since 2001 having had their combat debut in 2002 over Iraq.

Today, two squadrons of Super Hornets and two squadrons of legacy Hornets make up the primary combat power of the modern carrier air wing: almost 50 aircraft with the ability to perform both traditional fighter and attack missions. When a carrier attacks a target, the attackers are F/A-18s, the fighter cover is done by F/A-18s, the air defense suppression is achieved with F/A-18s.

Even the aerial tankers are now F/A-18s. When carriers respond to a crisis, the first aircraft across the beach is an F/A-18. The bottom line: these days, the Strike Fighter community is "carrier aviation."

A somewhat recent departure from the initial concept of having specialized aircraft types for each specialized mission around the carrier, multi-mission aircraft or Navy Strike Fighter Squadrons (VFA) have only been around since 1980. Before that, there were Fighting Squadrons (VF) and Attack Squadrons (VA).

There have been no VA squadrons since 1997 when the venerable A-6 Intruder was disestablished after 30 years of service, and there have been no VF squadrons since 2006 after the last flight of the world

famous Grumman F-14D Tomcats of VF-31 turned out the lights on the pure fighter community at NAS Oceana. Today, the Navy practically operates only Strike Fighters off the boat save for a few Prowler squadrons and Hawkeyes and helos of course.

When you look at strike fighters you are looking at a game changer. In the 1980s, people spoke of the "all-Grumman air wing" consisting of Tomcat fighters, Intruder all-weather bombers, Prowler electronic jammers, and Hawkeye AWACS birds. In the not-too-distant future we will be speaking of "all-Hornet air wings" where F/A-18s have replaced all of the fighter and attack squadrons, and EA-18G Growlers will have replaced the Prowlers. Only the Hawkeyes, CODS and helicopters will not be Hornet airframes. What the Navy calls "necking down" is another word for Strike Fighter.

"The end of the Cold War" is another way of saying Strike Fighter. In 1991, with the cancellation of the Navy's version of the F-22, the Navy had to find a way to get an interim fighter into the air quickly. They could re-open F-14D production, or they could build new Super Hornets. Secretary of Defense Dick Cheney wrote in 1991 that the Super Hornet had greater reliability and safety, required fewer maintenance hours, and had lower operational costs, in short, it was "the more cost-effective aircraft." Not necessarily the most capable, but with the collapse of the Berlin Wall and the search for a "peace dividend," the world's sole superpower had to watch its budget. But also in 1991, Hornets proved the meaning of the word Strike Fighter.

This is the view of lead and the Herc from Dash-2 over Newport Harbor. I'm sitting on the ramp directing the formation with a radio and a helmet and O2 mask to cut down on wind noise.

rlier in the season during the Rhode Island National Guard airshow at Quonset Point, we again utilized the incredible C-130J of the 143AW to make these images of a VFA-106 F/A-18C own by Lt. Adrian Jope callsign "CATFISH". As a single-ship formation behind the Herc, CATFISH was free to demonstrate the slow-speed maneuverability of the "Legacy" Hornet.

On the first night of Operation Desert Storm, two Hornets from USS Saratoga carrying four 2000-pound bombs, plus Sparrow and Sidewinder missiles, detected an approaching pair of Iraqi MiG-21s. Without even breaking a sweat, the two Hornets went to air-to-air mode and shot down the two MiGs, then went back to air-to-ground mode to deliver their 8000 pounds of ordnance on target. "Making it look easy" is another way to say Strike Fighter.

Perhaps the most important change in this period from the Hornet's perspective was the coming of age of precision-guided weapons in the early 2000s. Because the Hornet's genesis was in the 1974 "Lightweight Fighter" competition, it has never been known as a long distance, heavy load hauler. But today, an aircraft carrying a pair of laser-guided bombs or JDAMs has greater on-target lethality than last century's A-6 carrying nine tons of iron bombs. With these new weapons, going smaller does not mean settling for less; the Hornets and Rhinos are the right size at the right time. So Strike Fighter also means "digital-age warfare."

With the original Hornets setting such a high standard, the Rhino has lived up to the expectations placed on it. It is cheaper to operate and requires fewer maintainers and fewer all-nighters to produce an "up" aircraft. It has greater range and more payload than the legacy Hornet, is newer, and has a greater growth margin.

2005 saw the roll-out of the first Block II Super Hornet, with a new nose carrying the APG-79 active

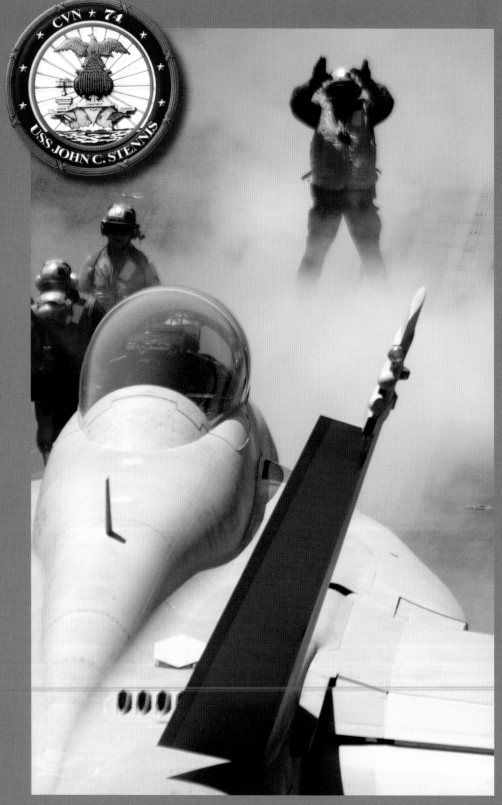

electronically-scanned array radar, capable of conducting simultaneous air and ground attacks. The Super Hornet is a fighter, a self-escorting ground attack or maritime attack aircraft, a self-escorting reconnaissance aircraft, a suppression of enemy air defenses (SEAD) aircraft, a self-escorting tanker, a self-escorting Forward Air Control-Airborne (FAC-A) craft. There's a reason why the Navy is buying so many, because almost everything a carrier air wing needs to do, the Rhino does.

So I could show you the real life jobs of the pilots and crew that we all see fly at airshows, I traveled out to the west coast and embarked the John C. Stennis in San Diego for a C DET or carrier qualification detachment. Seeing these planes and personnel operating as they were intended to is a very powerful sight indeed.

Currently there are 20 fleet squadrons equipped with the Rhino, ten each of single-seat Es and two-seat Fs. All 12 surviving F-14 Tomcat VF squadrons are now F/A-18 Rhino VFA squadrons, and legacy Hornet squadrons are also transitioning to the newer, bigger bird.

Strike Fighter is the future. The Navy currently has orders for 460 Super Hornets, and may order many more to make up for the inevitably delayed F-35C Joint Strike Fighter. Either way, American carrier decks will be launching and recovering strike fighters for as long as carrier decks exist. Yes, someday there will be unmanned combat air vehicles (UCAVs), but for as long as we live, there will be a need for men and women in the cockpit of fast, lethal aircraft.

We don't yet know what the Rhino's "personality" or legacy will be. It has not yet had its Final Countdown or Top Gun star turns. But in the hands of US Naval Aviators, it will have a reputation and legacy worthy of those at the brightest, sharpest tip of the spear. "Strike Fighter" is another way of saying the heart and soul of Naval Aviation for years to come.

Just prior to making the trip, I had purchased the then new NIKON D3 digital camera. It has an incredibly sensitive imaging chip that allowed me to capture these surreal night photos w only the light from the full "commanders moon". Lore holds that is was customary that higher ranking commanders would time their CQ periods around the phases of the fullest mo possible to provide for optimum conditions for coming aboard in the dark, in theory making is easier, but never easy. Photo of me on Vulturesrow by Frontline's John Alexander.

The two images on top were made while standing high on the front catwalks of the carrier's island. On the top left, you can see a series of three faint ghost images of the Super Hornet as it is shot off the number one CAT. At night, the Rhino's red anti-collision lights flash three times quickly while the Legacy Hornets only flash a steady on/off. This allows the LSOs to tell the difference at night between the two aircraft in the pattern, critical to confirming the proper weight settings on the arresting gear.

These last pages are both taken from the Golden Gate photo mission. Above, the formation made several 360 turns once outside of the bridge so this was shot looking west as we headed toward the coast. Opposite page is a similar right hand orbit off shore with the Monterrey Peninsula holding back the typical marine layer of clouds just west of Salinas.

US NAVY
BLUE ANGELS

They are the backbone of the industry. Airshows around the country hold their breath waiting to hear if their show has been selected as a Blue Angel show site. And if you have ever seen them fly, you know why. The Blues ROCK!

Essay by David C. Nilsen

Through ongoing experimentation with the Blue Angels year after year, we continue to try and capture never-before seen perspectives of their demonstrations. By chasing the Diamond and the Solos with a dedicated "floater", we are able to bring back images like these taken from above in BA #7 flown by ex-solo Len "LONI" Anderson. Opposite page shows Boss Mannix leading the Diamond through the Double Farvel with he and TORIS inverted.

Another view looking down as Corky blast towards his max-performance take off climb. Bottom left shows the Diamond "behind the crowd" off the beach at Pensacola. Bottom right shows the detached floater perspective inverted on the backside of the line-abreast loop. Opposite shows the Diamond clearing left behind the crowd.

They always fly at the end of the day: the last performance. It would be easy to say, "saving the best for last," but that would be unjust to the other performers, all of whom are among the best in the world at what they do. Instead of "best," let's just say, "those who have been doing it the longest." Since 1946—no aerobatic or demonstration team goes back so far—the Blue Angels have been working their magic across the United States and around the world.

This has been an amazing show. F-22s and Super Hornets have done handsprings and impossible turns and everything but bring us a beer. But still, those gleaming blue and gold planes have been sitting out there at Show Center all day, begging people to ask, "Those planes are gorgeous. When are they going to fly?"

They are perfect just sitting there, catching every ray of the sun, shining them all back, brilliant and pure, onto the crowd.

There is a day full of amazing flying and iron-willed feats of airmanship: hammerhead stalls, outside loops, free-falls and spirals and precision parachute landings, Old Glory and the Union Jack coming down under the boots of special forces soldiers, planes hanging on propellers past all likelihood of survival, wing-walkers, ribbon cuttings, all of these people are amazing, there is no denying it, and we are glad to have been here just to see them.

And still, there sit the blue and gold planes, like lizards on a hot rock in the sun, gathering their strength for a blinding, darting, spurt of speed.

Why are we here? When some of the young families with children, overcome by the heat from the beating sun bouncing off the concrete—not to mention the hot dogs and cotton candy and funnel cakes—have withdrawn to their cars, trailing diaper bags and souvenirs to beat the rush, why are we here?

We know why, but we don't know the words. We barely even know the thoughts.

Somewhere, deep inside of us, a caveman crouches at the mouth of a cave, flinching at the sight of the coming storm, the black clouds, the flashing lightning.

And now, down the flight line, come the vans and sedans at high speed, like a presidential motorcade through a treacherous city. And out pour dark-blue suited personnel, who gather around the blue and gold planes with a proprietary, protective manner. We instantly see that they know these planes; they've spent long, serious hours with these planes; they love these planes.

Somehow they and those planes are the same thing: human will and aluminum and steel and other metals forged into one goal. We don't know how we know it, but we know. They stand straight, in carefully arrayed lines. They are ready. We realize that we, too, are ready.

2008 is the 62nd Blue Angels season. Longer than most of us have been alive, the Blue Angels have been there...been there...doing what? "Demonstrating tactical techniques?"
Working sorcery?

No, they have been parting the heavens to show us a glimpse of that eternity which they and we serve. After all, they are angels.

Oh, God, we are proud. We apologize for our pride, but these airplanes are ours, and we are proud of what they are about to do. These are people like us who come from within our tribal borders, and we exult to call them our own, and cheer when they are from our states or commonwealths, but they reach for infinity, they reach for you. Six men in blue and gold uniforms march precisely from one end of the flightline to the other. They are perfect and precise, and yet human. We know this by the way they shake the hands of the dark-blue men who defend and guard these planes. They are easy and casual, yet confident. They climb into the cockpits, and we know the thrill that they feel for what they are about to do. We know that we don't own this moment, we only bear witness to it. But we are part of it. We are here. Today. Where it is happening, and will never happen again. We are here. We brought our children. To see it. To live it. To bear witness to it.

These are the Blue Angels. They are blue, as any child of the Navy should be, but they are also angels, something magical, something beyond us and our understanding, something divine—and yet something that is here, with us, that we can participate in.

And before we know it, they have leaped, like some four-limbed beast, into the air and formed their shape that we know in our hearts, and still thrill to see.

And we are here, and they are here, and this is happening, and it is now.

Why do we love it? Why do we know that it is part of us and still beyond us? The Blue Angels have a name that is simple, and at the same time unfathomable. Blue is a color, but what are angels? We know that they are brighter and higher than us, and yet they speak our language. They beckon to us to follow them. Somewhere in the back of our minds we also remember that "Thunderbird" is also an eternal, supernatural creature. There is something going on here that

Opposite page is a look-down perspective through the line-abreast loop with NAS Pensacola below. Top this page shows the view from the ground of what a "detached floater" photo chase looks like. Thanks to Tom Callahan for that shot. The bottom shows the Echelon roll from the #4 jet with TORIS at the Duluth Monaco Air airshow.

This page shows an interesting moment frozen just as TORIS initiates the 6.5G PUB or pitch up break. You can see our shadow in the sun-dog / glory spot with the remaining Delta formation yet to break. Opposite page shows the reverse angle of exactly the same moment that I shot the next day from the ground at the Duluth show.

we are part of, and yet still strive for. And we are glad to be here.

The caveman is at the mouth of the cave, watching the oncoming wall of clouds, seeing and feeling the lightning strike. He is nothing; he knows it. He retreats into his cave, knowing the thrill of wanting to be alive, even though something is coming that could kill him, should kill him, but which thrills him all the same.

The blue and gold planes fly. We hear the shriek of the air parting at their passage, we feel the rumble of their power in our chests; we know what it means to be in that cave.

We normally imagine that we have conquered this world with our wheels and our gears and our chemistry and our high-bypass turbofan engines. And yet what we really yearn to feel is that we are part of something that is bigger than us, can still frighten us.

The $21 million planes crisscross the sky singly and in unified shapes made from four or five or six pieces. On a normal Saturday-Sunday airshow weekend, the Blue Angels will require 40,000 gallons of fuel. (Don't worry, the entire Department of Defense consumes just 2% of the United States' oil consumption each year.)

What does wonder look like? Is it the diamond or five-abreast line carving figures in the sky above us? Or is it the fact that you are one of ten thousand people united by the act of looking up at the same point in the sky at the same time?

Nearby, older couples scream and laugh with delight at the "Sneak Pass," 700 miles per hour of blue and gold guile. They have learned their lesson: they will watch the sky, they will not be surprised by lone planes again. But by watching attentively, they appreciate all the more the carefully synchronized comings and goings of the six planes above.

The crowd begins to cooperate. Photographers with impossibly long lenses blink at the sky, "where did they go?" And helpful members of the crowd call out to the photographers and the old couples, "There's the diamond, and the solos are out there." Although we've never met each other before, we are now united in...experiencing something, and realizing while we are doing it, that we are all doing it together.

When we see them on this weekend, they have already been here for two or three days, because this is not easy. In the words of John F. Kennedy, we choose to do these things "not because they are easy, but because they are

hard, because this goal will serve to organize and measure the best of our energies and skills." They arrived on Thursday, and on arrival conducted three hours of what they refer to as "circle maneuvers." It is here that the pilots first survey the surrounding terrain, pick out the landmarks, and designate the points on the ground that they must avoid, and where they will begin to execute their maneuvers and join up again afterwards.

On Friday they had their formal practice show, usually for local dignitaries and veterans and dependents groups. They also use Friday to take up a member of the local press in Jet 7, and watch to see if he'll puke. (Sometimes they'll also take up a talented photographer.)

On Saturday and Sunday, it's work. Make no mistake. It is hard work to make this stuff look so natural and fluid. These are six people, remember. And they'll sign your program after they land. But somehow their flight suits will still have razor-sharp creases in them. Only angels can have such good dry-cleaning.

There is nothing so good as sitting outside on a summer afternoon with a hot dog and a drink, unless it is sitting outside with a hot dog and a drink while looking up and being amazed, and moved, and thinking, "These are my guys. This is my United States Navy, these are my F/A-18 Hornets, and I participated in some way in preparing this team to be here today. I am an American; they protect and defend me, and they represent my Navy. And I'm glad for it, and proud."

Why do we love it? For those of us who've stayed to watch this last, most spectacular show of the day, there are a couple hours of traffic jams getting out of this place. Why do we do it? Why do we know that this aerial expression is worth it; is part of us and still beyond us?

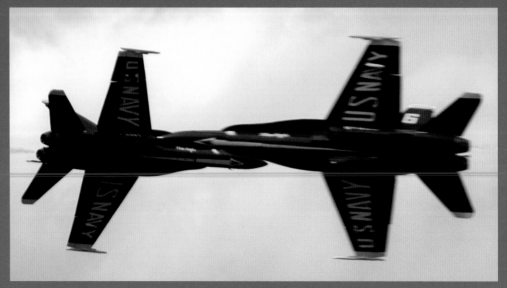

Top this page shows the echelon pass in review at Pensacola. Top right is the line-abreast flat pass shot from the ground. Bottom two frames are simply interesting moments from the same show at Duluth. Opposite page shows what it looks like inside a cloud during the Diamond Dirty Loop as we go over the top during the Friday practice in Duluth.

The caveman, braving the sheets of rain and crashing thunder and strobing lightning, creeps back to the mouth of the cave. He must see this thing that is happening around him, that somehow involves and yet frightens him. This world is his world, and yet it is bigger than him. But if it were not bigger than him, why else would he love it, why else would he be part of it?

We love it because we are there with them. Yes, we are on the ground and they are in the air, but our spirits rise to join them in the beauty and precision and power and audacity of what they do. And they invite us to do it with them. We see raw power and performance in the hands of professionals, who know how to use it, who respect it and love it, because this level of accomplishment cannot be reached without loving it. And they cannot love it without us. Because they are there to represent and defend us, in the best way they possibly can. They are there because there is a nation, because there is an us, to give meaning to their dedication and to create the body that they work for.

And the caveman stood through the lashing rain, and watched as the thunder and lightning passed over him, onto the next range of hills. And he knew, finally, that these things that were bigger than him, to which he owed his fear and respect, were still part of his world. And if they were a part of his world, they were also a part of him. The lightning in the sky and the lightning he then drew on the wall of the cave are, at heart, the same thing.

And that is why we love these six planes in the sky: Because it is something we participate in: it is all of us together; it is what we shall become, and which we can see a glimpse of now: a spark, a distant blue-and-gold gleam of where we are all going: to be with the angels. We are here now only a moment on the ground, but we shall be forever with the angels. And we saw some of it today. And they sang to us, and beckoned for us to follow.

It is six men in blue and gold flight suits.

It is six gleaming blue and gold airplanes.

It is a few dozen men and women in dark-blue coveralls, guarding and nurturing those planes, and a whole organization of dozens and hundreds more who make it all possible, and a nation of millions for which it exists, and for which it will give its life.

This blue and gold diamond in the sky is why we are here; it is what we are; it is who we are. And we are here: today, now, always.

We are proud to be here. How could we be anyplace else?

This page shows the results of one of our experiments with LONI to see the Team from new and interesting angles. This is the fan-break away from the crowd at Pensacola. Opposite page is the view from the Slot with TORIS of Boss Mannix leading the Diamond down the show line during the Double Farvel at Duluth... very close and very loud!

RED BULL AIR FORCE

An invite-only fraternity of canopy pilots, the Red Bull Air Force is one of the most creative demo teams on the planet. When you put together a team of all-out wild-men with an average of 14,000 jumps each you get some pretty entertaining situations.

Essay by Luke Seile

Dog-pile on the Twin Beech! Do you think these guys consume much product?

Getting by with a little help from their friends. The boys always take the time to enjoy every second of a demo, especially when it means inspiring next generation flyers. Most of their demos have a lot of action but a high speed swoop always makes people stop and take notice.

The Red Bull Air Force is a unique blend of paragliders, skydivers and B.A.S.E. jumpers; a grab bag of canopy piloting skill combined with pure insanity. The paragliding contingent consists of two of the most experienced and well rounded pilots the sport has ever seen. Masters of both the Cross Country and Aerobatics disciplines, Othar Lawrence and Chris Santacroce both men have trouble keeping their heads out of the clouds; Santacroce, once reached an altitude of 20,000 using his knowledge of wind and thermals.

The biggest motivator for both Lawrence and Santacroce isn't being innovators in the sport, it's sharing the stoke. Lawrence explains, "My mission is to spread the word that airsports are the most engaging, challenging, and fun sports imaginable, with the most creative playing field available: three dimensions!"

Where the paraglider's skill creates the look of grace, the B.A.S.E. jumper's confidence gives the appearance of pure insanity; enter Miles Daisher. While all the members of the Red Bull Air Force partake in the guilty pleasure of B.A.S.E. jumping no one has done it to the level that Miles has. Daisher lives in a small town in Idaho called Twin Falls which contains one of the few legal B.A.S.E. jumping sites, the Perrine Bridge. The bridge combined with Daisher's endless supply of energy has allowed him to amount 2361 B.A.S.E. jumps at the time of this writing. Of course that number is ancient history by the time you read this as he hopes to add 365 to that number in 2010.

While the Red Bull Air Force contains canopy pilots from all disciplines the majority of their 75 plus demonstrations each year put skydiving front row center. Composed of World Record holders, National and World Champions, they are innovators in modern skydiving techniques and equipment. Each member has their own specialty within

This tight-knit band of brothers has known each other for so long that it is hard to tell which they enjoy more, their time in the air or their time together on the ground. Even the majestic backdrop of Monument Valley, Arizona is no match for the wrecking crew.

the facets of skydiving, skills that originally brought them to the forefront of skydiving. The Red Bull Air Force includes a group of athletes that were largely responsible for the discipline of freeflying, a technique that updated skydiving from the strict belly down format. With freeflying, skydivers began to realize that they could fly their body in any position imaginable; spinning and flipping or stable head down. But what really separates the team from other demo teams is their canopy skills.

The entire team flies small, high-speed parachutes that allow them to swoop the ground at close to 65-miles-per-hour; their precision allows them to land on a postage stamp. Skydiving ambassador and unofficial team therapist, Jon DeVore explains, "Skydivers at our level are hands-down the fastest non-motorized machines in the world... AND we can fly with more precision than most aircraft."

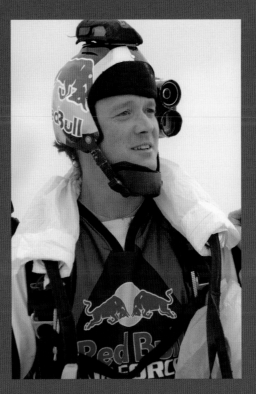

CHUCK AARON
RED BULL HELICOPTER

To fly aerobatics professionally takes a mastery of precision, steady nerves and years of experience. To do aerobatics in a helicopter takes a pilot that is just a little bit twisted.

Essay by Luke Seile

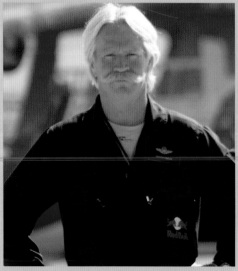

Chuck Aaron is the man controlling the stick in the Red Bull Helicopter. Aaron is crazy enough to try almost anything in the highly modified BO-105CBS, and talented enough to pull it off.

As a child, Aaron had a recurring dream about flying a magic carpet out his window to see the world. That dream combined with inspiration from his father, his hero, who flew fixed wing aircraft in World War II, Korea and Vietnam, gave Aaron the motivation to create his own magic carpet. His lifelong dedication below a rotor head reached a pinnacle when he became the first pilot to be licensed to do aerobatics in a helicopter by the FAA.

Since that time Chuck has been flipping his helicopter and turning heads all over the country while pushing the limits of what is possible in a helicopter. Chuck's relaxed demeanor isn't a façade. With the call sign "Malibu," Chuck looks as comfortable in flip-flops and shorts as he does a flightsuit.

When this cool character starts flying, the Red Bull Helicopter is his office and he is there to do work. "My dream came true. I'm flying my magic carpet," says Aaron. "And my hope is to inspire children to come up with their own aviation dreams, and to give them the wings to make it happen because dreams do come true."

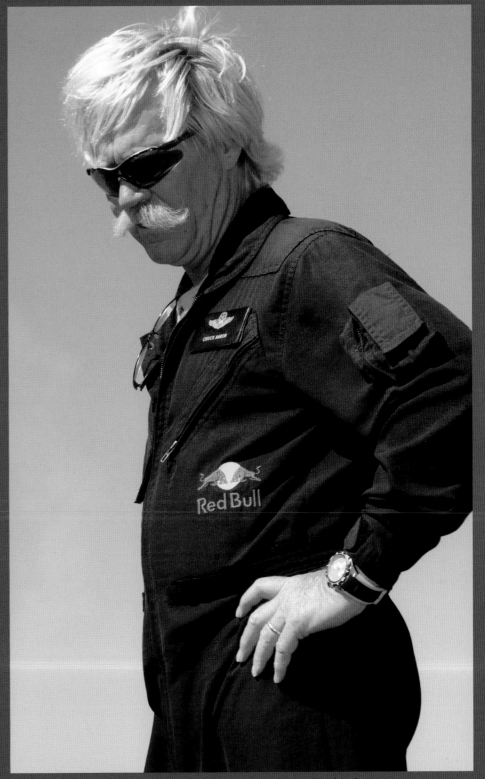

A man on a mission; Aaron is out to prove to the world that the right helicopter and pilot can do everything a plane can. With his family behind him he continues to live his dream. Wife Wendy and daughter Ashley visit with Malibu before he buckles in. With Stan Gray and Luke Seile as crew, Aaron is able to focus on being a helicopter rock-star.

Chuck "Malibu" Aaron and members of the Red Bull Air Force blow away all the other acts at the Aviation Nation Air Show in Las Vegas.

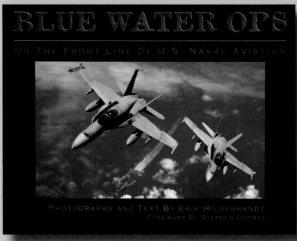
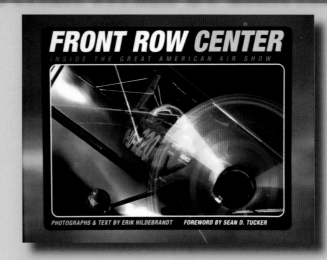